I'M TOTALLY KILLING YOUR VIBES

Ahren Warner has published three prevous books of poetry with Bloodaxe, including *Hello. Your promise has been extracted* (2017), which was shortlisted for the Roehampton Poetry Prize 2018. His debut, *Confer* (2011), was shortlisted for both the Forward Prize for Best First Collection and the Michael Murphy Memorial Prize 2013. His fourth collection, *I'm totally killing your vibes*, was published in 2022. His books have received three Poetry Book Society Recommendations and awards including an Arts Foundation Fellowship. He works across writing, photography and moving-image, with an intermedia project, *The sea is spread and cleaved and furled* published by Prototype in 2020. He was selected for Bloomberg New Contemporaries 2020 and his work has been exhibited at galleries and institutions including TJ Boulting (London), South London Gallery (London), Saatchi Gallery (London), Centro de Cultura Digital (Mexico City), Nikola Tesla Museum (Zagreb) and the Great North Museum (Newcastle).

AHREN WARNER

I'M TOTALLY KILLING YOUR VIBES

BLOODAXE BOOKS

Poems & photographs copyright © Ahren Warner 2022

ISBN: 978 1 78037 602 8

First published in 2022 by
Bloodaxe Books Ltd,
Eastburn,
South Park,
Hexham,
Northumberland NE46 1BS.

www.bloodaxebooks.com
For further information about Bloodaxe titles
please visit our website or write to
the above address for a catalogue.

Supported using public funding by
**ARTS COUNCIL
ENGLAND**

Cover design: Neil Astley & Pamela Robertson-Pearce.

Printed in Great Britain by Bell & Bain Limited, Glasgow, Scotland, on
acid-free paper sourced from mills with FSC chain of custody certification.

for Elle

ACKNOWLEDGEMENTS

Some of these poems have previously appeared in *Poetry London*, *Prototype* and *Test Centre*. *The sea is spread and cleaved and furled* was first published by Prototype (2020). The text of *The sea is spread and cleaved and furled* was developed from the voiceover for a moving-image work, *I'm thinking what would sound sincere, but also, like, oh that's super cute* (2019), selected for Bloomberg New Contemporaries 2020 and exhibited at the South London Gallery (2021). *Serviced Living* is developed from the text for a film exhibited as part of a solo show, *We have a space for your every mood*, at TJ Boulting (London, 2022). I am grateful to Arts Council England, A-N Freelands Foundation and the Society of Authors for funding that enabled the completion of this book, and to Vahni Anthony Ezekiel Capildeo, Jess Chandler, Sophie Ruigrok and Mark Waldron for their critical advice, influence and indulgence.

CONTENTS

The sea is spread and cleaved and furled   *9*

I'm totally killing your vibes   *43*

Serviced Living   *85*

THE SEA IS SPREAD AND CLEAVED AND FURLED

Are you happy, she asks. i'm happier, i say, and then: if you had to be an animal, which animal would you be.

She cannot fit her mouth around the English for the animal she means. Have you ever been happy, she asks.

She means a swan. She likes the way it wraps the long elegance of its neck around its lover until, like, forever.

i don't think i've ever been happy, i say. And then: if i had to be an animal, i'd be a zebra.

A zebra is just a horse with stripes, i say. i can tell she was hoping for something more profound.

I was hoping for something more profound, she says. In front of us, two cats are rolling on what used to be the grass.

The cats are rolling in the heat. Beyond, the ground gives to cliffs, it gives to the Tyrrhenian sea.

I think too much, she says, it's one of my problems. Let's play a game, i say. My skin itches on raw heat.

What type of game, she says. Let's make a list of all our problems, i say. You go first, she says.

We drink meloncello for breakfast. i make a silent list of my problems. i am thinking which ones would sound

like bare sincerity, i say. i'm thinking which would sound, like, super vulnerable. i'm thinking which would sound

sincere, but also like, *oh, that's super cute.*

You're a good me, i say. That dude with the gut behind the counter, he's a bad me, i say. She's snoring gently.

She's a good me snoring with elegance. The man with the gut brings coffee. Cardi B is a good me, i say.

Leonard Cohen is a good me, although he's dead, obviously. Michel Foucault is a bald me.

Foucault is a bald me that looks like Doc Brown. Michael J Fox is a metaphor for my own inevitable decline,

in the sense that another's misfortune is, actually, always about me.

Chris Brown is a terrible me, i say. She is wearing my underwear, she is purring like a hedgehog.

You snore like a hedgehog, i say. She is embarrassed. The taupe of her cheek flits rouge.

This is what i want, i say. What, she asks. To watch you blush, i say. The sea is cold, and we

are so very drunk. The sea is cold and she is not here. The sea is cold and we are spread out on a hot rock.

The sea is spread and cleaved and furled by the relentless heft of a tanker.

i am on a tanker and a drunk Estonian rigger is sleeping on my shoulder. i am on a ship sidling into Sicily.

i am on a ship that grinds and bumps against the Spanish waves. i am on a ship watching the water break

and acquiesce and sew itself back together again. That's what i want, i say. What, she asks.

i want to feel you give, i say. That sounds hot, she says. You're always thinking about sex,

i say. Will you sew me back together, she says. Probably not, i say.

And then, i say, are any of us really anything other than gaping wounds. Are any of us more

than a patch of weakened bone. That's dark, she says. i know, i say, and then: i only love my bed

and my mama, i'm sorry, i say,

because citing North American hip-hop artists is something i do, i say, it's something i do

to ease the tension, it's something i do with the kind of irony you should read as sincerity, i say.

This isn't cynicism, she says. No, i say. Or if it is, i say, it's also love.

It's also love, i say. It's also love, in the way your boot on the head of a kitten you've doinked with your fender

is a kind of love, i say. In the way, sometimes, when you're making a hollandaise sauce and it splits, you launch

the electric whisk so that the plug snaps right out of the wall, and the whisk crosses your open-plan kitchen,

the whisk spins and glides and spanks the living-room wall, and you pick up the whisk and you kneel down,

and you start to thrash and gash the antique parquet floor until it splinters and the whisk is little more

than mauled plastic, and the sawdust of the floor is beginning to float gently in the tiny puddles of your hot tears.

It's a bit like that, i say.

Your tears are hot, i say. Thanks, she says. i like tears, i say. Thanks, she says, looking down at my

erect cock. It's not tears themselves, i say, it's not that i have a fetish for salted water,

a lachrymal kink. It's not the sadness, either, i say. Sadness is an unfortunate bedfellow of tears, i say.

No, i like the fact of a dam breaking, i say. That's a cliché, she says. Ok, i say, i like how tears feel like an oesophageal sphincter

giving, i say. Tears are like delicate eye-vomit, i say, in the way that puke is the unfortunate bedfellow

of vomiting, i say. You like to vomit, she says. It scratches an itch, i say.

i am itching at my skin. i am itching at the insides of my arms. i am itching at the backs of my legs,

i itch until my skin deepens to a red beyond this ridiculous British sunburn. i am itching until

my skin is a polkadot of hives. i itch until i bleed, until pin pricks give to errant drops that smear

across my thighs. She is drinking her espresso, slowly. She is talking about swans. She places her hand

on mine. She moves my hand away from the particular patch of skin i am mid-way through shredding.

She places her palm as a cool salve on this patch of half-flenched skin. She curls her fingers into her soft palm.

She runs those tiny, milk scythes against my arm. She runs the nails of both hands against the length

of my arms. She is itching my calves, she is digging her nails in. She is smiling sweetly as she

bleeds me. i am fizzing. i am humming, thank you.

Thank you, i say. She is not here, she is not here to say, 'you're welcome', in that way that both demurs

and says, 'damn right'. She is not here and i am sat on a hot rock, i am sat on an inflatable flamingo, i am floating

out to sea, i am floating towards the Albanian coast and the sky is clear and all i can see is the full moon

and the furcle and fizz of sea foam. A Dutch boy is unconscious, he is snoring on a sunbed as i trudge in

from the sea and place my wet, inflatable flamingo on the sand. The Dutch boy is barely eighteen.

The German girl by his side is twenty. The German girl is singing let's go to the beach, beach,

let's go to the beach. And i say, but we're already on the beach, and i make a slow

mournful gesture towards my flamingo.

The gestures of mourning, i say. That's a good title for a poem, i say. I don't think so, she says,

and i gesture to an inflatable flamingo with the closest i can manage to puppy-dog eyes. You're always

pointing to your damn flamingo, she says. And she's right, of course, she's always right. i spend my life

as a drunk Italian stag on an all-you-can-drink boat tour, necking complimentary

shots, and drinking something that has once been described as Prosecco.

i am wandering the dance floor, i am pacing in ever smaller circles, i am wearing a large

inflatable flamingo around my waist. i am pointing to its long, pink plastic neck protruding

from my crotch. i am pointing to my flamingo in the hope you don't look at my face.

[A country wrapped in militarism, a country dug into autocracy. A bridge on which tanks are wont

to park themselves: as coup d'état, as show of force.] There is a nearly new-born kitten outside the window.

She is not here. The kitten is making the exact noise one might expect of a stuffed toy.

She is gazing out of the window. It is a nearly new-born kitten, she says. It's dying, she says.

That's the problem with stray cats, i say. They're everywhere, but so are their mouldering corpses.

i want to take the kitten milk, i say. i want to spoon it, hushing: *it will all be OK*. It won't, she says.

i want to cup that kitten in my hands and bring it to our bed, i say. The hotel would have a problem with that, she says.

i want that kitten, i say.

and then: i roll over, i tuck myself into the one position that almost always brings the soft descent

of sleep. i am forcing myself to sleep. i am counting dead and dying kittens, i am counting undead

cats, i am counting zombie felids scampering, and bouncing, and making the sound a cat might make

if it had smoked a couple of packs every day of its nine lives, if a cat had puffed woodbines

like a cat-like beagle, like a cat who has sidled off to a hedgerow or roadside bramble to die a lonely death before

being stuffed and rigged with wires and having its sternum cracked to be fitted with a small plastic box

that makes the noise a cat might make if it were not, in fact, a cat, but the digitally enhanced fact

of my own pain.

Of your own pain, she says. Yes: the kittenish squall of my own pain, i say. And then: she laughs,

she rolls her eyes and puts her finger and thumb together like Steve Buscemi in *Reservoir Dogs*. She is playing

the smallest violin in the world, she is gesturing to the absurd depths of my sullen self-indulgence.

But it feels so good, i say.

It feels so good, i say. Really, she says. i'm not sure you're properly accounting for my #emotionallabour, i say.

She is demonstrating very little interest in my emotional labour. In fact, she is demonstrating an emphatic lack of interest

in my emotional labour. i am good with that, i say. With my disinterest, she says. Well let's be blunt, i say: you and i

are really the same person, aren't we. She is nodding. A little disinterest might be healthy, i say.

For someone who finds themselves so compelling, she says. i am nodding. i am not really listening,

i am thinking about Cardi B. i am thinking about how i am a rich bitch and i smell like it. i'm in a boss bitch mood, i say,

and these are boss bitch shoes.

These are boss bitch shoes, i say. She is making the exact sound
a gerbil might make, if the gerbil was trying to lift

a relatively heavy weight. A ham sandwich, for example, a ham
sandwich larger and heavier than the gerbil on which it sits,

a gerbil trying to squat-lift its own weight, along with the heft
of a thick-cut sandwich, constituted largely of bread

and ham, and the slightest scraping of a particularly delicious
dijonnaise. It is a noise that sounds pretty much

like a squeak. It is a snore. She is squeaking and snoring and
dribbling lightly on my chest.

Our taxi is skimming the Bosporus, slowly. Her hand is absently
pummelling and pawing at my crotch.

i am hot and hard and alone in a cab with a middle-aged man
called Mehmet. Do you think Mehmet can see

how horny i am, i say, how obscenely jacked and awfully desirous
i am. And alone, she says. Yes, i say, and alone.

We can all see that, she says.

You're terribly alone, she says. i know, i say. And then, i say, aren't we all, at bottom, just wrapping ourselves

in others, in their cuddles and kisses, and spooning in the rapt haze of dawn light, our only free hand

moving from their knee to their hip with a slight twist at the mid-point bringing our fingers slipping between

their thighs as a very gentle good morning, that leads to an incrementally firmer how did you sleep, as they turn

and nibble sloppily on your bottom lip, until they open their eyes and one of you enters the other,

much like how the Sartrean subject exists only in the eyes of another, much like the way Drake sings

baby, you finer than your fine cousin, and your cousin fine, but she doesn't have my heart beating double time,

but it's only his own heart that beats.

Is that your heart beating, i say. i feel myself cringe. We are spread out on a hot rock rising from a shallow bay

between Naples and Sorrento. Our clothes are bunched and sullied among the pebbles and boulders on the shore.

What is this all about, she says, are you just fucking with me. Yes, i say – i place her arm around me

and snuggle up – i'm totally fucking with you. But also, i'm not.

She is suggesting a second defensive line of poison. i am spraying a second defensive line of poison

between the old oak stable door and the second, interior door that is made of glass and steel.

We are digging in, we are waiting for the cockroaches' dusk offensive, when they swarm up from sewers

and scuttle along the old slabs of the Palermo pavement, when they charge under the doors of our Airbnb

as we are upstairs and one of us is going down on the other, or we're spooning in the glow of a Netflix Original Drama,

until the lull of sleep and the vicious light of morning and i am sent down with an aerosol of poison

and a boxfresh sneaker and our defensive lines have not held, but have limited their advance

to a few dozen roaches pitifully trying to drag themselves towards our bowl of Cantabrian stonefruits

and i am at last the vengeful god i've so often dreamt of being, and i am slapping my boxfresh sneaker down

and i am splatting and spattering and shouting *die motherfuckers, die* and they are dying with a crunch and a spurt

of their entrails, of the frothy egg-white of their young who are nothing but spawn, but who will hatch soon enough

and come for us in the hot fug of night.

Tonight is a super hot fug, i say. What is a fug, she says. That's difficult to say, i say.

We have paid a krunked Italian man with a very small car and a questionably-cropped denim jacket

to drive us back to the city. She is sat next to him, i am sat behind her, i am pressed against

a middle-aged Hungarian woman who once worked in B2B telesales. Our B2B saleswoman

is squished against a former US marine who has seen the business end of her penchant

for snorting sambuca. He is covered in his own vomit, he is sat behind our monumentally shitfaced driver.

The driver speaks at an alarmingly rapid pace. She turns to tell me that he is refusing to stop the car

unless he gets her number. i giggle; she is worried. i'm not worried, i say: we have a US marine

and he's sat behind that krunked motherfucker. He could wrap his brutish arms around our driver's neck,

i say, he could whisper 'don't struggle', like Jack Bauer, in episode after episode of hit 2000s TV show, *24*.

He could whisper 'don't struggle' as some enemy combatant, some spy, or – in fact – our monumentally shitfaced driver,

refuses to comply, then flails and jerks until he sinks softly into the benevolent violence of our ex-marine's arms.

Our ex-marine is sobbing uncontrollably. He is knocking his head into the back of the driver's headrest.

He is clawing at the driver's headrest.

The sea is spread and cleaved and furled, i say. You've said that before, she says, you're starting to repeat yourself.

The sea is spread and cleaved and furled, i say. By the relentless heft of a tanker, she says.

Yes, by the relentless heft of a tanker, i say, and by the small diesel-powered skiff we've borrowed for the day, and filled

with Antipodean millennials and crates of *Mythos*, until its hull sits a little lower than the Albanian gent who rented it to us

would like. That's true, she says. And by our own bodies, i say. You mean by your own body, she says.

i do, i say, the sea is spread and cleaved and furled by the stuttering heft of my own body, by the whip and flicker

and chunk of my own legs, and by the spread and drag of my oddly spindly arms that heave the weight of my recalcitrant heart

through the waves. I know, she says. i swim like a sad hippo, i say. Without grace, she says.

Yes, i say, but with the plump, grey certainty of getting my own way.

i like getting my own way, i say. Don't we all, she says. You really want me to tie you up, i say.

I do, she says. But what should we use, i say. She is gesturing at the towelling belt of my dressing gown.

i'm not sure, i say. Why, she says. i'm not sure these hotel gowns are 100% cotton, i say.

i feel like it might be a polycotton blend, i say, and that could be unpleasant. Unpleasant is what I like, she says.

That's why you're here with me, i say. It is, she says. She is crossing her wrists behind her back.

She is turning away. i am tying her hands behind her back. She is turning towards me.

i'm not sure, i say. Why, she says. i feel like you're performing a role for my pleasure, i say.

Are you enjoying it, she says. i am, i say. Are you happy, she says. Enjoyment and happiness are not the same, i say.

I know, she says, but are you happier. i'm happiest when i'm enjoying myself, i say. How long will that last, she says.

i'm not sure, i say. i'm trying to perform the vacuity of my own self, i say. Why, she says. Why not,

i say. And then, i say, have you ever thought about how, when Drake sings *take that fucking dress off, I swear you won't forget me.*

You tell me you're just not the type, you wanna do this right, but... does waiting really make us better people?

He's really just another iteration of Marvell's *But at my back I always hear, time's wingèd chariot*

hurrying near; then worms shall try, that long-preserved virginity, and your quaint honour turn to dust...

i think about it often, i say.

I live it, she says, and it's not very interesting.

i think about it often, i say. About what, she says. The sea, i say.
Oh, she says, stirring her tiny coffee

with a tiny spoon. It is six in the morning and two men in high
visibility jackets are turning a massive cog

and a massive coil of rope is unfurling, and slipping into the sea.
i am sipping a tiny coffee and eating a tiny

chocolate croissant, and licking the salt and sweat and the odd
pépite of chocolate from my upper lip.

i am shivering, i say, to no one, or to the sea, or to a self that is
almost entirely a network of conjectures

about a certain person's thinking about me. It gets to a point, i
say to this loose filigree of conjectures that are just about

hanging together, where you can't tell if you're slapping another's,
or your own, face, it gets to a point

where you want to slap yourself so hard, you think you find
yourself slapping another, and then you think you're slapping

another, but you're tearing strips from your own face.

i am tearing strips of jackfruit from a jackfruit taco at a vegan fastfood eatery, because vegan

is in, and jackfruit is the new catch-all vegan feel-good meat substitute for people like me

who like the dirty slip of something akin to flesh, and more cashew-mayonnaise than is possibly

good for them, but who also enjoy the semiotics of their own moral rectitude nearly as much as the food.

So, is that a problem, i say. For who, she says. Is it a moral failing, i say. It is, she says, although

in the world we live in, it's hardly up there is it. Up there with what, i say. I don't know, she says, perhaps

genocide, or sex trafficking, or the systemic oppression of women. That's a fair point, i say,

and this jackfruit is delicious.

i was staying in LA and the jackfruit was delicious, i say, and the farmer's market had the most wonderful array

of speciality peaches, i say, all laid out by variety, with sample slices for each type arranged perfectly on a tray.

She is giggling, gently. What, i say. I'm just wondering if you're aware of how you slip so easily

into self-parody, she says. i'm aware, i say, slipping into self-parody. i'm aware that i am sat at a small ornate table,

alone, facing a smallish mosque, picking at a small plate of tabouleh as, somewhere, the muezzin

issues his call to prayer. Where do we go from here, i say. We keep going, i say.

We keep going, i say. Why, i say. Why not, i say. Shall we talk about Freud, i say. Do we have to, i say.

We do, i say. And the 'death drive', i say. OMFG, what is your problem, i say. Why can't you just

leave the artifice of your own learning at the door, i say. i can't, i say. It's kind of like brain damage, i say,

it's like the patient who recovers from hypoxia but who will always tremble or forget certain names, i say.

OK, i say, but keep it brief, i say. i've always felt a certain affinity with Freud's description of the death drive, i say.

Blah blah, i say. Of the drive to destruction, to darkness, to a nothing that is also the only way

of quelling the terrible excitation of living, i say. You're such a bore, i say. That's true, i say,

but what i'm saying is also true. OK, i say, so why keep going.

So why keep going, i say. Because of this, i say, gesturing beyond
a few rocks to a couple of crabs

scuttling and stopping to bathe under a late Sicilian sun. i am
slipping my hand into her hand and curling

her fingers into my palm. She's not here, i say. i know, i say, but
the tears streaking my face are real, i say

and so is the way my neurons are shivering with something i have,
in the past, called love, i say. That's fair, i say,

but is it enough, i say. It is, i say. Even if you're alone, i say, even
if you're dawdling and dithering and floating

from one shore to another, endlessly partying and forgetting what
it feels like to inhabit your own face.

It's not ideal, i say, but it's a bed of my own making.

I'M TOTALLY KILLING YOUR VIBES

a man i have met twice has taken a dislike to my latest book. it seems he is quite

narked, or narked enough to write about it in a periodical of some reputation.

LOLZ. huge LOLZ. i am alerted to this by Twitter. my girlfriend wakes to find me chuckling

heartily. my girlfriend is less amused. she dislikes his charge of misogyny, she dislikes my use of the word *sluts*

being taken for what Judith Butler might have called *the public display of injury*.

i dislike my citation of Ginsberg and Yeats being taken for original lines. *i am not that good,*

i say. *he should really be better read if this journal wants to keep its reputation*, i say.

and then, LOLZ. and then we really laugh, because the man i have met twice seems to think

what he writes matters, that writing matters, that anybody really cares or reads what he or i write,

and that is, like, super LOLZ. silly man, we say. *though he does have a poem about ponies*, i say,

and my girlfriend rolls her eyes.

We are in the hallway of our small apartment. The hallway is also a kitchen and we are making soup. The left half of my face does not work. There was a brief moment when we worried I might have had a stroke, but the internet told us it was Bell's palsy. We are eating the soup, you are sat on the sofa, I am sat in an armchair. The soup goes in the side of my mouth that works, much of it goes out of the side of my mouth that does not work. You are giggling, beautifully.

My three earliest memories all involve a kind of descent. In one, I am failing to run down a staircase, flailing and stumbling and falling as a popular toy – a fluorescent green ball made of plastic suckers – pursues me. In another, I am terrified of my own inability to descend two steps clad in frayed beige carpet. Finally, I think I recall being held close to my father's chest as we slipped rather slowly down what must have been an incredibly tame water slide.

Michael has given me a very bad review. this matters, i say to my girlfriend, and then:

Airbnb is built on mutual trust, it's our new model, it's kind of like *Blanquism*, but less French

and about making money, and based on the web instead of in, like, nineteenth-century Paris,

but Michael's very bad review of my stay in his 'cozy flat close to city centre' matters

and although i didn't leave it in pristine condition, it was a shit-hole anyway,

and i want to amend my original review, in which i had demurred and suggested

that Michael's 'cozy flat close to city centre' was adequate, and i want to edit my review

to say *fuck you, Michael, fuck you and your hipster collection of Coltrane and Jacques Brel vinyl*

but, i can't. i can't do it, because i wrote my review first and these are the Airbnb terms

that i signed up to but didn't read, because who even reads the terms and conditions,

and Michael says *i could have left the apartment cleaner*, and now i am nothing

but a slovenly shit, nothing but a disgusting, sloppy splotch on the virtual realm,

which, because it has been written, is also a kind of truth.

The morning is near silent, a communal hangover is draped across the campus. Outside, chicken boxes and kebab wrappers slink through the courtyard. We have given up on the single bed of my student halls, we are wrapped in each other, we are a tangle spread against rough, blue carpet. We are both crying and tears are running and pooling in the folds of our skin. There is a hard slant of light that reaches between the curtains, it runs against the side of your waist, your right hip, the top of your thigh. I am an appendage. I love you.

Martin is a bigot. This morning,
his snore and stutter startled me.

As a student, Martin lived in Brussels.
You hear so many languages there,

but mostly Arab. Martin wants to visit
all the major European cities.

He has been to Bucharest. He sweats.

I tried to tell you this once. Although I admit I did not say it clearly, and in fact I hid it in a rather oblique sonnet, stowed behind allusions to Freud and learned obfuscation, which I now regret completely. So, you may have missed it, but: for as long as I can recall, I have rather disliked myself. I admit that a half-feigned sense of superiority, the ease with which I dismiss others, may have obscured this fact, but they are not mutually exclusive possibilities. It is possible to hate yourself *and* to hate others.

Marvin is on his fourth wife, she is Ukrainian.
They want him for his money, so why not buy them?

Marvin does not care for Marx's critique of reification.
You say: *Marvin, you're a tool*. Marvin says:

seven figures a year feels better than six.

the ageing burgher of Blackpool from whom i have bought a vintage 28 millimetre lens, says

i'm an AAA++ buyer. and i think, *that's* who i am. i'm an AAA++ buyer. and i slip and slither

into the bathroom of this once grandiose Ukrainian hotel to check myself out in the mirror,

and i take off my boxers and socks so i can see the entirety of my AAA++ buyer's bod,

and i admire the way the scales on my strange reptilian muffin-top glint and glitter in the twenty-five watts

that flickers on, and off, and on to reveal my delicious tail and my complete lack of nipples

and i extend the rather significant length of my forked tongue, which is also my nose,

and i lick and sniff the length of this smeared and flaking Soviet-era mirror,

and i lick and sniff the length of my own reflection, and i shiver and trill at the taste of iron

and coca and strychnine, which is also the taste of myself, which is also the taste of money.

The internet is chit. Marco has a girl back home,
a girl he's been trying to argue with for days.

His girl's so angry that he won't argue with her.
Marco is so angry, but he can't argue with her

because the internet is chit. Marco says,
It's Friday night and sometimes you just need to dance,

sometimes you just need to fuck.

How many bathroom floors have we picked each other up from? This one is different. You are not sick, I am not drunk. I am balled up full foetal and my face is slick and gunked with snot that I smear as I bawl against the tiles like a massive, whining snail. You have prised me from the floor and you hold me to your chest and my eyes and nose and mouth are smearing snot and tears against your chest and you do not care. I am soiling you, and it is making everything worse.

After everything, after months of giving me more than I deserved, you have told me it is over. I am sat in the antique German armchair with an inset pegging effect on its teak legs that we paid too much for because of the inset pegging effect on its teak legs, which is considered collectable. I am sat in my studio and the studio manager lets himself in to discuss repairs to the ceiling of my unit to find me sat in an antique German armchair, staring at a property website, tears drizzling my cheeks.

As a child, as a pre-adolescent, I spent all of my pocket money on a birthday present for a pretty girl that did not like me. I remember my father telling me that this was nice, but that a girl needs to like you, and it does not matter what you buy her. I am thinking of this when I ask the studio manager to leave, when I pick up the phone to ring an estate agent, when I view three properties the same afternoon; when after five minutes in the last, most expensive, I take it without bothering to make an offer.

I am convinced that the only way to make things better is to be a better person, to be the person that you will like. I spend months crying in our old bed, fucking Tinder dates in our old bed, hurrying random strangers through rushed avocado-based breakfasts and out of the front door, so I can continue to cry in our old bed.

I am trying to show how much better I am. I am trying to be the functional human that I hope so much you will like again.

the Poet Laureate of the State of Oklahoma does not like my new book.

'this is not how Celan does it,' writes the Poet Laureate of the State of Oklahoma.

and i think: *no shit*… and then i think: how *does* Celan do it?

and then, i think: *hairless, and with the unbleachable stain of living.*

It is the morning after a night in which I very nearly slept with a woman who works for me. It is a running joke that she would like to sleep with me and I won't, because she works for me. Instead, I invite her back to my apartment on regular occasions and very nearly sleep with her. In the end, all's we do is sleep.

This morning she asks, rather plainly, *why* I won't sleep with her. And I say something to the effect of not wanting to take advantage of her. And she calls out, rather plainly, the misogyny of this position, its erasure of a space for her own agency, for female desire.

You're right, I say, affirming my own gross misogyny. I do not tell her that I do not feel it as such, or that I assume somebody sleeping with me is both *out of their minds* and a victim of my own, very male, violence.

Maria works at the hostel. Before the current regime,
abortion was legal for victims of rape and women

at risk of dying. Now, even if Maria was *raped
and had her legs cut off, she must have the child.*

Maria has a friend who lives in the same town
as N—— F——. Maria says *N—— is a drunk,*

he often stumbles around asking where he is.

Of all the batshit crazy things I said to you on those nights we talked and cried and talked again, until I left our flat unable to bear the batshit crazy things I was saying, was that I did not know if I still loved you. That was a lie I told because I wanted you to hate me, because I'd slept with another girl and in the act of confession the oddly thin canopy of my own self that I'd spent years propping and patching up as a protection from my own self, was whipped away and I was left with nothing but my own self, a self I could not let you love. I never stopped loving you.

Mick took the wrong tram twenty minutes south,
and then the right tram forty minutes north,

to fire guns. Mick studies drama. He owns
several paper men drilled with bullet holes.

Here, Mick says, *is the rifle. Here, is the AK-47.*

Ms A Brooke, who self-identifies as a middle-aged hag and Essex girl who writes fantasy novels and gay short stories

has given one of my books a single, lonely star. this, it seems, is at the opposite extreme

to her review of the first volume of the authorised biography of Margaret Thatcher, *an excellent biography*

of a woman who is a particular heroine of mine. such reverence offers a rather severe contrast

to my own work, which is *pretty much pretentious and shallow...* which is not as *clever*

as it thinks it is. Apparently, there were *one or two moments where,* Ms Brooke thought, *a real poet might be emerging,*

but it actually never happened.

We are eating ceviche. This is what we do now, we are people who both live in Shoreditch and meet semi-regularly to eat ceviche, or sometimes gluten-free waffles from a hotel lobby in which one can also procure healing crystals.

We are not here to procure healing crystals. We are here to eat ceviche in a semi-regulated manner, which amounts to the forced maintenance of a friendship that we have both professed to value. I find our consumption of ceviche deeply upsetting, although I understand the need for boundaries and the semi-regulation of our new dynamic.

I am clearly *killing your vibe*. You are going to Reykjavik at the weekend and the awkwardness with which you gulp on a particularly small cube of tuna ceviche tells me that you are not going to Iceland with friends. We finish our ceviche, I finish my drink. I will not ask you a question you do not wish to answer because the least I can do is to stop being a cunt.

We walk the Bethnal Green Road and you stop to tell me you are going to Iceland with a guy. I say: I know. We agree we should discuss it at another of our semi-regular meetings. I suggest we do not do it over ceviche.

I leave your flat and walk the Bethnal Green Road, crying and snotting like an oversized toddler. I can see that you are healing. I think that I will keep these tears to myself. Perhaps, I will keep them in one of the many kilner jars I have unwittingly inherited from our life together. Perhaps I will keep them in a jar, with my heart, diced into a salted heart ceviche.

at the Q&A that follows the screening of a short film i have made,
a tall artist with an intensely critical practice

remarks that much of the film relies on the footage of a certain
architectural style.

baroque and rococo palaces, i say. the tall, critical artist would like
to know

if my film is providing a critique of certain hegemonic structures.
i am perplexed.

i nod politely. i suggest he is correct. *the thing is*, i say, *i despatched
a messenger-boy by stallion*

*to request a tête-à-tête with the appropriate Habsburg, in which i
thought we might politely discuss*

the radical reallocation of wealth in eighteenth-century Mitteleuropa.

*the relevant Hapsburg declined, because he is dead. so i decided to
make a film.*

We are in our apartment, I am staying elsewhere. I say I am feeling better. You say that is good. You say that it feels like the first time in months that you can recognise me. We kiss. I take a taxi back to my rented room. I am careful not to wake the girl I am renting from as I walk through the house, stroke her cat, close my door and undress. I resume my usual position, knees clutched to my chest, sobbing and wrenching at my own skin.

Where we ever happy? There were so many days that felt like boundless pleasure. But, when we first met, you were not a happy person. I spent a long time doing a very good impression of a happy person. There is a Leonard Cohen song in which he growls *We've been alone too long. Let's be alone together. Let's see if we're that strong*. I can no longer bear to hear his voice. I have not been able to hear his voice since the night I left our apartment and lay in a hotel room trying to drink myself to sleep or dead and did not care which and walked the Tower Bridge looking at the Thames, at its spangle and glitz.

Matthan grew up in Exarchiea. He studies law.
Sure, there is no work in Greece, and sure:

the EU screwed them. But that's not our problem,
Matthan says, *the problem with the Greeks*

is that they're lazy. They don't go to college,
when they go to college: they drop out.

Matthan is never going home.

I am in Venice and I am speaking about you to a friend.
I say we are trying to stay friends. She says that she
could never be friends with someone she loved. She
says it would be too painful. I hear myself say: that's
the point.

We are seventeen and staying in a Paris hotel. My poems have earned a surprising amount of money. I have an unfortunate tendency towards the grandiose. I have taken you – my girlfriend of a few months – to a city with which we are both enthralled.

We have decided to try the jacuzzi. I have never been in a jacuzzi. Neither of us have swimming attire because the hotel I booked had rooms with ornate fabric wall-paper, but no jacuzzi.

On arrival, the travel agent had fucked up our booking, and the hotel with ornate fabric wallpaper sent us to a hotel that is markedly less ornate, but with a jacuzzi. Hence, we are sat in a jacuzzi and the boxers of mine that you have borrowed are ballooning ridiculously around your painfully small waist.

our 'critical friend' has completed his reading of all the department's potential research outputs

for the upcoming 'research excellence framework' assessment, in which the 'research'

of departmental staff wholly or fractionally on research 'contracts' will be assessed.

our 'critical friend' has declared my own outputs likely to be judged 'world-leading research'

in terms of 'originality, significance and rigour'. six-feet below, the corpses of Turing and Leavis are turning.

further down, somewhere around the fifth or sixth circles of H, E, double-L,

senior management are hunkered and purring, and rubbing their hands, and already sketching plans

for new buildings to be built in an identical style to buildings that have recently been built,

but with even bigger 'break-out' spaces, and even less human warmth, and even more PVC furniture,

and a shrine dedicated to eternal risk assessment, and a modest inner sanctum adorned with 3D-printed

idols, in which all of us – senior manager, financial officer, professor and fixed-term lecturer –

will strip naked and engage in a prolonged and 'rigorous' circle jerk, before setting light to a bonfire

of students' cash, and students' dreams, and the last vestiges of whatever we once

called our souls.

the independent bookshop i like very much has started to follow me on Instagram.

by which, i mean, a very beautiful and painfully modish woman who runs it

has started to follow me on Instagram. following anyone on Instagram

is also a form of affection. the beautiful and painfully modish woman

likes me, i think. she likes me, i say to myself. and then i think of how well-connected

she is, how many launches of obscure photography monographs she hosts,

how many events for cult, but highly-influential fashion magazines.

and i think how she likes me, and i think: maybe this means we could meet IRL.

and i think how she might introduce me to the editors of cult, yet highly-influential

magazines. and i shiver and beam at the promise of being at the centre

of a six-page editorial, of nothing but me, and me wearing those Balenciagas,

the ones that look like socks, and rye, erudite captions that say:

'ahren is wearing a Dior tux and those Balenciagas, the ones that look like socks,

as he lounges on an Eames-inspired, custom-made, beige velvet podium

and discusses Proust with a small, Bengal kitten named Lydia.'

For years, you used to tease me by telling others the story of how we met. A new year's party organised by members of my sixth-form. You were there with a friend, although you went to another college. Your friends' parents picked you both up and took pity on a boy who was near hypothermic and who they liked because he once chaperoned their daughter to a concert.

I was *wasted*. The father of our mutual friend handed me a large, wooden salad bowl to chaperone for the journey. I turned to you and slurred something I intended to be saucy about the size of my salad bowl. This is ridiculous. It is almost certainly true. It is not the first thing I remember about you.

The morning after, you came downstairs in our mutual friends' house to find me hungover and trying to recall the evening before, staring blankly at cartoons with our mutual friend's sister, who asked you why men sit with their legs so far apart. You smirked and whispered loudly: he's a *boy*, and he wants us to look at his cock.

I'm not sure I ever told you this: I went home that morning and broke it off with a girl I had been torturing for months with my petulance. I will never feel as enraptured as I did.

You tell me in an email that you hope I will not close my heart to meeting someone new. I do not reply, because I know you do not want me to. I believe we have an honest disagreement. I believe I had a sizeable, but ultimately limited, supply of love. I gave you all I had, and once I ran dry I found myself with nothing but tear-fuelled nights, and days of incredible rage.

Vahni Capildeo has written an extended review of my latest collection of poems.

Vahni Capildeo is one of my favourite poets, so this is a BIG DEAL.

this is a pretty big deal, i say to my friend, of this review of my latest collection by Vahni

Capildeo that i still haven't read. why haven't you read it, my perplexed and very short

friend inquires. and i say: i lose hours each day with my finger hovering over the clicker

and the unclicked cursor hovering over the hyperlink that will take me to the page on which

i am concerned that Vahni Capildeo has laid my inadequacies bare. i spend much of each day

immobile. i have fallen and landed in an overrated Kubrick film, in which, as always, i'm the star,

and Vahni Capildeo has placed callipers on my eyes, and Vahni Capildeo has forced my eyes towards

a screen on which Vahni Capildeo has bound my hands and placed me on a large, lustrously

gilded, fish smoker. Vahni Capildeo is smoking me like trout, and when I am smoked

Vahni Capildeo takes an unusually strong thumb and equally unyielding finger and Vahni Capildeo

is pinching me just below my pelvic fins and curling away the crisp of my skin, and Vahni Capildeo

has taken a fish slice to the pink of my flesh, has pulled away the first of my fillets, is teasing my spine, is lifting my skeleton from what's left of my body. And now Vahni Capildeo has snapped my spine

from my disembodied head and that unusually strong finger and thumb are pressed inside the back of my fish skull

and my trout eyes and trout lips fill the screen as Vahni Capildeo moves a finger and thumb

together and apart, so my trout lips are moving like a talking trout, and i'm little but the bodiless head

of a smoked trout miming the words, *i'm bad, you know it, really really bad, you know i'm bad,*

i'm bad, though without the fishiest hint of irony, and my trout face is mouthing *shamone*

as unutterable confession.

I am working in the States. You are in Galicia. I left the week after we moved into an apartment that has more rooms than we could possibly need. You have been sleeping and eating and reading on an ikea mattress waiting for the movers to bring everything we own, all of which will fill slightly less than two of our many and various rooms. We are speaking on Facetime. Your colleagues are terrible human beings. You are telling me how the older of the two movers asked you to marry his son, we are laughing. I am in Rhode Island, and after I hang up, a poet I love and who will later die suddenly in her sleep is getting me drunk. I say I have been with my girlfriend for ten years, that we met at seventeen. She cocks her head and purrs, *oh baby*. I know *exactly* what she means. I smile. I sip at my drink. She is wrong. She is dead, but she is still wrong.

Maurice is a club rep. Maurice is super hungover.
Last night Maurice took a girl home at eleven-thirty.

Then, Maurice came back to the club.
Maurice took a girl home at three a.m.

Maurice has been speaking to me for thirty seconds.
His dick *itches*. He wants me to know this.

It is New Year's day, the evening before was your birthday. We spent it together watching films, me unable to do more than hug you without risking a panic attack, without risking another evening of being a *total drag*. I have landed in Mexico City, I have been bundled into a car by my driver and driven north into the night. I am at a hotel that was once a monastery, in which I will spend a week teaching old, rich Americans how to marginally improve their poems. I will spend a drunken night with one of their drunken daughters. I will spend almost all of each day crying in my room. I will stop only to teach workshops, give tutorials, or to drink.

It is New Year's Day. It has taken weeks and I guess I still do not believe we are over. Later, you will tell me you told me. I will tell you I did not understand. The day before was your birthday. I spent it in my apartment, it is the first in fourteen years we have not spent together. I slept it away, and now I am running. I am running the Kingsland Road, and London Bridge. I am running the Southbank and Westminster Bridge. I am running Hyde Park and the Mall and Embankment and Smithfield. I know now I have been running since the day I blew everything up. It's only when I stopped, when I wanted so badly to come home, I realised you had given up.

Martina has problems. She's done the Ayahuasca
and it was really, really super,

though she did it properly, in Peru,
and she couldn't drink or have sex for, like, ever.

Martina has also been to Cuba.
She has ridden a scooter the length of Vietnam,

but now she is back in Milan, and so are her problems.

Days after the night I left our apartment and moved into a beige hotel on Tower Hill, I am sitting in the kitchen of a friend. He and his wife have both had affairs and they keep telling me to work it out and feeding me spaghetti puttanesca. His wife has gone to bed, he is making me tea, he is asking me what I am going to do. I can see that he sees that I am utterly broken. He says: ok, but you are going to be very unhappy for a very long time. I say: I am aware of this.

Marzena is really very helpful. She sees my camera
and asks if I care for postindustrial architecture.

Marzena draws a map of two abandoned towers.
She draws triangles for two guardhouses.

She adds an arrow to where I can jump the fence
without entering the guards' line of sight.

In addition, she suggests a district I might like.
Marzena says, *it is very interesting, it is very poor.*

It is Christmas. We are living in Paris and it is the first time we have escaped the obligatory festive tussle between our respective parents' homes. You are walking in front of me in a woollen coat that your boss has given you out of pity at the sight of you blue-nailed and shivering. You are turned three-quarters towards me, the sky stretches out behind you, gnarled grey and split and riven with fantastic light.

I am thinking of a Leonard Cohen song, of his haunted, tender drawl: *It's four in the morning, the end of December. I'm writing you now just to see if you're better.* I know you are better. I know you have gathered the pieces of yourself and arranged them into something better. I am not surprised.

I am writing to say I am *better*. I am writing to say that I am so pleased that you have a new life, and it is better than your old, and it only tangentially includes me. There is a song by Rainbow Kitten Surprise, in which Sam Melo sings: *I'm not hurt I'm broken, but I called to say I'm fine.*

I'm fine, because the pain and the rage and the heartache are real this time. I am pleased because I still love you, I am still in love with you, because only one of us should feel like this and it should, of course, be me.

I am writing to say: I miss you, I hope you stay as far away as you need to.

SERVICED LIVING

How are you? Do I care? If you say, 'I'm fine, thnx',
what do I get out of it? I've been worrying lately that I
have a hashtag-problematic relationship to *limerence*.

A dead poet once said: Plato was right to define the bodily
pleasures as the pouring water into a hungry sieve, but
wrong to ignore the rhythm which the intercrossing, coloured
waters permanently give.

You shouldn't believe everything poets say. Often, they're just fucking with you.

A dead poet once said, I need your surface company *(what happens below the surface is my own affair)*.

That's a good line. I've thought about using it on Tinder. I find that allusion is often under appreciated. I like to tell girls on Tinder that I like *cats*.

I LOVE CATS

Yet, I'm aware that exhibiting what is perceived as sensitivity and then being a total asshole appears to have a causal relationship to getting laid.

Yesterday, I was reading something and there was a link to something else and then that thing had a link to something about Jordan Peterson, who I know *very little about* except, that at certain kinds of party, performing a radical disdain for his philosophical position seems to have had a causal relationship to getting laid.

On occasion, performing a hashtag-problematic openness to Jordan Peterson as part of a broader commitment to *intellectual plurality* seems to have also had at least a positive correlation to getting laid.

I once had the misfortune to hear Jordan Peterson arguing that a multivariant analysis delegitimises the notion of a gender pay gap created by less sophisticated univariant analyses.

I know it's awful, but I found myself thinking how nice it was to hear the word *multivariant*: how delicious that pivot from alveolar stop to the soft slip of a vowel inching up your palate.

How are you? Do I care?
If you say, 'I'm fine, thnx', what do I get out of it?

Postmodernism has taught me that I get very little out
of it.

I *really do love* postmodernism. Even though I know it's no longer *on trend*, and this particular concatenation of the past passing into the passé, reminds me of my own unease, that internalised necessity to souse all intellect in a marinade of irony and…

…here we are. This is *who* we are, and we have *amenities*. There's a French verb, *amener*, from which the English 'amenity' does not, like, *actually derive*. Does that matter?

Amener, meaning 'to bring', 'to take'. For example, you can 'amener' your Italian Greyhound for a walk. *Amener.* You do it to something, you do it with force. Much as, if you're amenable, you can be brought, you can be taken, although the implication is that it will take very little force. Unless force is your thing, of course.

Do you have an Italian Greyhound? That would be, like, a *total plus*.

Here, we have a swimming pool, if swimming is your thing. We have a sauna and a steamroom. On the twentieth-floor, there is a bookable room within which you can be *zen*. It is called the 'zen room'.

We have co-working spaces, we have cinema rooms, we have a room called the playroom in which nobody seems to be very playful.

How are you? If I ask you if you want to play, and you say 'yes', what do I get out of it?

I want that tremor in your voice, I want a 'yes, please', I want a *please* more chemical demand, more 'please me', more 'please, me', than politesse, than well-mannered assent.

There's what we *want* and what we *have*. Here, we have a library stocked with books of *almost no interest*. We have velvet sofas softer than the furred space between a cat's nipples.

I FUCKING LOVE CATS

Some have asked if this is a kind of cynical affectation, an offset for my, admittedly hashtag, toxic brand of masculinity, much as I read that Blackrock and Goldman Sachs are hedging their extractive stocks with some kind of vague commitment to eco...

It's, like, *totally not*.

Here, we have a rather well-stocked gym. But, you know what? Whilst I'm pumping that 180lb bench press (not a lot, I know, but I'm working on it, man, I'm working so hard at getting hashtag-stacked), the only *real* thing pumping through my arteries is a deep, sincere love of cats.

There's almost nothing I don't like about cats. But, perhaps one of their most attractive aspects is their *whiskers*. Have you seen how they twitch?

I want you to twitch, I want you to quiver, I want at
least the implication of a slight caterwaul, when you
say: *yes, please*.

When you say you hate globalised capital, do you
really?

Does anyone really hate global capital? Except, perhaps, the Congolese kids (yes, some as young as six), digging cobalt down a mine somewhere close to Lake Malo?

I'm pretty sure those kids – the same ones you're fucking over every time you swipe right, the same ones I'm killing every time I type '*dtf?*'... I'm pretty sure those kids would hate global capital, if anyone had taught them the particular euphemism currently in vogue for their hashtag-infant-misery.

Anyway, *that's a drag*. Let's get back to that which is at hand. This sumptuous velvet sofa has its lustre enhanced by the diffuse light offered by an understated brass lamp. Do you like it?

If you say, 'Yes, I like it', what do I get out of it?

There's what we want and what we have, and by some estimates the gap between the two is what we call desire.

Except, if I've had you and I still want to have you, that's what we also call *desire*. And, yes, I know the idyll is we'll grow old together and …

I don't desire the 'Blades of Light' intermediate healing crystal – even if it comes from Colombia and comes with a handy reference card describing all its key healing attributes, even if it's a very friendly quartz that would be happy to come home and work with me to stimulate my loving consciousness and balance not one, in fact, but *all* my chakras – if I already have a Blade of Light intermediate healing crystal.

And yet, it's perfectly possible, is it not, for us to roll away from each other soused in each other's fluids and, still, what?

Desire each other?

It's not just possible, it's even considered preferable, at least in societies that place a premium on monogamy and the nuclear...

Here, a premium is placed on luxury, on convenience.

A cleaner – always female – will visit your studio once a fortnight. She'll replace the old organic Egyptian cotton bedding with freshly laundered organic Egyptian cotton bedding, devoid of the spunk and ketchup and ear wax stains that, at least, are a small expression of your own embodied existence within an otherwise rather inhumane world.

Of course, it's *awks* to hang around whilst she's cleaning, so what I do is I ride one of the four lifts to the ground floor and say hello to the concierge as I pick up a fresh copy of the *FT* and have a cheeky handmade dumpling from the handmade dumpling café…

If you say, 'I'd like a handmade dumpling', what do I get out of it?

I'd like to hear you say 'I'd like a handmade dumpling' in your most ASMRy voice whilst you slip off your bra and let it land lightly next to a conveniently placed microphone that can record the near silence of it folding itself into a crumple against the carpet's polypropylene pile, transmitting its soft hush as a paresthesic quiver.

And when I say, 'I'd like to hear you say 'I'd like a handmade dumpling' in your most ASMRy voice whilst you slip off your bra and let it land...' I mean, really, you can be saying *whatever you like*.

And when I say *I'd like that*, I mean: *please, do it*.

I mean, *do it*.

p.s.

i have been sending these poems to Wayne. i have been sending these poems as screenshots

interspersed with low-resolution, sexually explicit, Fine Art GIFs

i have been making in Corfu and Naples, in Palermo and Marseille, in Burgas, Milan and Berlin.

Wayne Holloway-Smith says they're 'fucking funny, like hahahaha', Holloway-Smith says

he 'likes the comic momentum, and the incipient anxiety produced by your need for validation'.

Wayne says 'you demonstrate an impressive level of self-reflexivity'. But, if i publish them, Wayne says

'everybody will hate you'.